Start-Up

Connections

AND

ENT

Claire Llewellyn

Evans

First published in this edition in 2010

Published by Evans Brothers Limited
2A Portman Mansions
Chiltern Street
London W1U 6NR

Produced for Evans Brothers Limited by
White-Thomson Publishing Ltd.,
+44 (0) 843 2087 460
www.wtpub.co.uk

Printed & bound in China by New Era Printing
Company Limited

Editor: Dereen Taylor
Consultants: Nina Siddall, Head of Primary School
Improvement, East Sussex; Norah Granger, former
primary head teacher and senior lecturer in Education,
University of Brighton; Kate Ruttle, freelance literacy
consultant and Literacy Co-ordinator, Special Needs
Co-ordinator, and Deputy Headteacher at a primary
school in Suffolk.
Designer: Leishman Design
Cover design: Balley Design Limited

British Library Cataloguing in Publication Data
Llewellyn, Claire
    Forces and movement. -- (Start-up connections)
    1. Force and energy--Juvenile literature. 2. Motion--
Juvenile literature
    I. Title II. Series
    531.1-dc22

ISBN: 978 0 237 54172 9

Acknowledgements:
Special thanks to the following for their help and
involvement in the preparation of this book: Staff and
pupils at Elm Grove Primary School, Brighton, Liz
Price and family and friends, Christine Clark and family.

Picture Acknowledgements:
Chris Fairclough Colour Library 14; Ecoscene 6, 7 *(top)*;
Popperfoto 7 *(bottom)*, 15 *(bottom right)*; WTPix 10.
All other photographs by Chris Fairclough.

Contents

Move that body!

We can move our body in all sorts of different ways.

▼ We can stretch our arms.

▲ We can swing one leg and then the other.

move   body

▼ We can **bend** at the hips and touch our toes.

▲ We can lift one leg and **balance** like a dancer.

How many different parts of your body can you move?
How many different ways can you move your arms?

stretch   swing   bend   balance

How does it move?

Things move in many different ways. We use all sorts of words to describe them.

▶ Look at this picture of a snake. These words describe how a snake moves.

Can you think of another animal that moves like this?

slither
stretch
slide
glide
wriggle

How do cats and birds move?

Which of these words would you use to describe them?

flap fly jump leap

soar stalk

creep swoop

flutter

Can you move like one of these animals?

glide walk run pounce

flap swoop creep flutter pounce ....7....

On the move

Alex is getting on his scooter to find his friends in the park.

▼ When he **pushes** his foot against the ground, the wheels **turn** round, and the scooter **starts** to move.

▲ Alex wants to go **faster**. He pushes his foot down **harder** and faster. He is moving **quickly** now.

pushes   turn   starts   faster   harder

▼ **Alex wants to turn right now. What does he have to do?**

▶ **Alex has found his friends. How did he slow down and stop?**

Let's pull!

Pulling is a way of moving things. We pull on a hat when we put it on.

▼ This water skier is being pulled along by a boat.

A pull is a kind of **force**. It makes things happen.

pulling   force

◀ **Many things in this kitchen can be pulled. How many can you spot?**

What would happen if you gave this plug and these apples a pull?

Let's push!

Pushing is a way of moving things. We **push** open a door.

▶ We push cymbals together to make them **CLASH**!

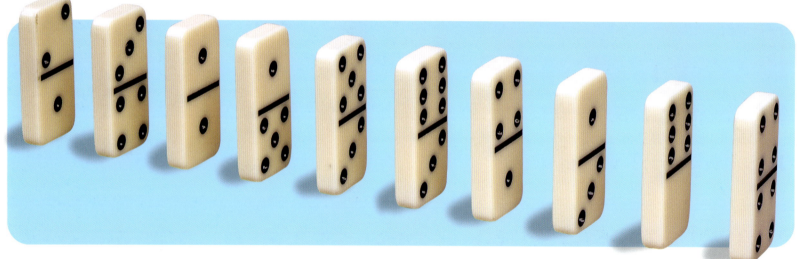

▲ A push is another kind of force. It makes things happen. Look at the dominoes in this picture. What would happen if you pushed the first one?

push   clash   wind

Wind and running water can push things. They are forces, too.

▲ What is the force pushing this washing?

▶ What happens when Patrick puts his water wheel under the running water?

running water   water wheel   13

In the playground

▶ Hanif is swinging high on the swing. It goes **forward** and **back**.

▼ Archie and his friends are on the roundabout. It's spinning **round** and round.

▼ Robbie and Nita are on the see-saw. It goes **up** and **down**.

How could Archie make it stop?

How are they making the see-saw move?

forward back round

How do the things in these pictures move?

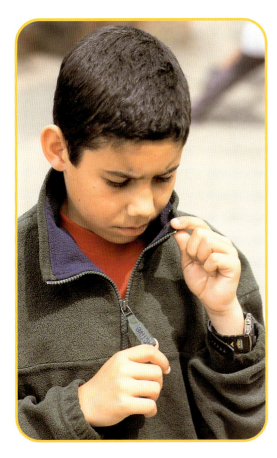

up   down

Rolling along

Becky and Ruth are playing skittles.

Becky rolls the ball along the ground. But she pushes the ball too gently… it does not knock the skittles down.

▶ Ruth pushes the ball much harder. The greater force makes the ball roll further. It knocks the skittles down.

rolls   gently   greater

▶ Morrissey rolls a marble on a carpet, on grass, on concrete, and on sand. He tries to use the same force each time. He **measures** how far the marble goes and writes the results on a chart. Where does the marble roll best?

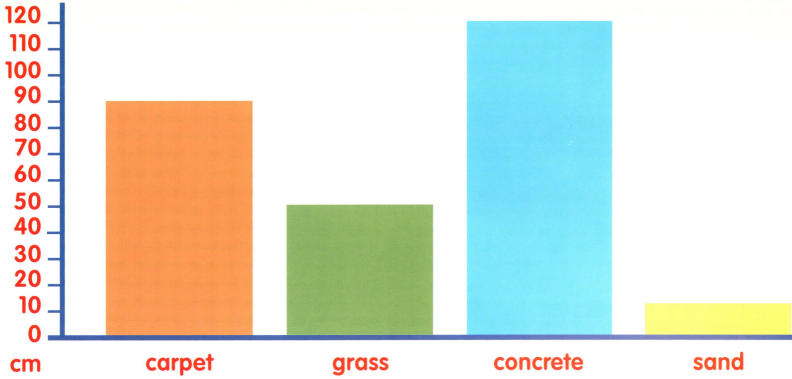

Make it stop

Tom's little sister is playing with her buggy.

The buggy rolls away.

▼ Tom pulls it back to stop it.

A force can slow things down. It can make them stop.

It is safe to stop things if they are light. It can be dangerous if they are heavy.

Which one of these two objects would you be able to stop if it were racing towards you?

Which one is too heavy?

What would happen if you tried to stop it?

Changing shape

Josh is making a snail out of play dough. He pulls and pushes the dough to **change** its **shape**.

◀ First, he makes a thin strip.

▶ Then he **curls** it to make the shell.

change shape curls

▼ He pulls off some different-coloured dough to make the body. How does he make the horns?

▲ Latha is making a long, wriggly worm. Her worm might **break** in two. Do you know why?

break

Further information for Parents and Teachers

FORCES AND MOVEMENT ACTIVITY PAGE

Use the activities on these pages to help you to make the most of *Forces and Movement* in your classroom.

Activities suggested on this page support progression in learning by consolidating and developing ideas from the book and helping the children to link the new concepts with their own experiences. Making these links is crucial in helping young children to engage with learning and to become lifelong learners.

Ideas on the next page develop essential skills for learning by suggesting ways of making links across the curriculum and in particular to science, numeracy and ICT.

WORD PANEL

Check that the children know the meaning of each of these words from the book.

backward	faster	joint	roll
balance	finish	movement	slower
bend	force	pull	start
change	forward	push	stretch

DEVELOPING VOCABULARY

Take children to the hall to explore different ways of moving.
- Establish their basic vocabulary of speed and direction: *forwards, backwards, sideways, fast, quickly, slow, push, pull.*
- Can they walk in different ways: *tiptoe, stride, stumble, stamp, creep, stagger, trip, plod, trudge, sneak, pace, saunter*? And can they *dance, hop, skip, run, race, sprint, hurry, speed, dash*? Talk about why people move in these ways and what each tells us about how people are feeling.
- Introduce names of animals and ask children to move like the animals. Develop their vocabulary of words to describe how the animals can move.

MOVING CHILDREN

Explore how the children's own bodies move. They can work in pairs to watch each other move and observe directions and kinds of movement. If you have any children in the class with physical disabilities, use your knowledge of your children to determine which activities are appropriate.

- How many places in their bodies can they bend? Are all of the bends in the same direction?
- How many places in their bodies can they roll? Do all of these places roll in the same direction and to the same degree?
- Ask them to think about how their bodies would be different if they couldn't, for example, bend their knees or arms at all and if their thumbs just bent like their other fingers.

MOVING TOYS

Either collect toys from around the school, or ask children to bring in toys from home - including toys for younger siblings.
- Give children opportunities to explore a range of toys, trying to find out everything that they can do. (You may need to remind children about respecting the toys so that they are not tested to destruction.)
- Children can take photos of the toys using digital cameras. They can then annotate the pictures with symbols to indicate how the toys move.
- Ask children to consider which forces they had to use to make each of the toys move: *push, pull, twist, press, slide, roll, turn, lift* They can add the new information to their annotations.

CARING MOVEMENTS

Read books which show caring relationships, both between children and from adult to child. Use the pictures to identify movements and forces which are associated with caring relationships. Be sensitive to, and prepare for, the possibility of safeguarding disclosures.
- Give children copies of the books, as well as pictures showing caring relationships. Identify movements which are associated with these relationships and the contexts (eg pushing a pushchair, clapping, hugging)
- Recognise uncaring relationships and identify movements which are associated with them (eg pushing someone over, hitting, squeezing)
- Discuss the idea that we can use our bodies for both kinds of relationships. Make reference to the school rules and focus more on caring relationships.

USING FORCES AND MOVEMENT FOR CROSS CURRICULAR WORK

The revised national curriculum focuses on children developing key competencies as

- successful learners
- confident individuals and
- responsible citizens.

Cross curricular work is particularly beneficial in developing the thinking and learning skills that contribute to building these competencies because it encourages children to make links, to transfer learning skills and to apply knowledge from one context to another. As importantly, cross curricular work can help children to understand how school work links to their daily lives. For many children, this is a key motivation in becoming a learner.

The web below indicates some areas for cross curricular study. Others may well come from your own class's engagement with the ideas in the book.

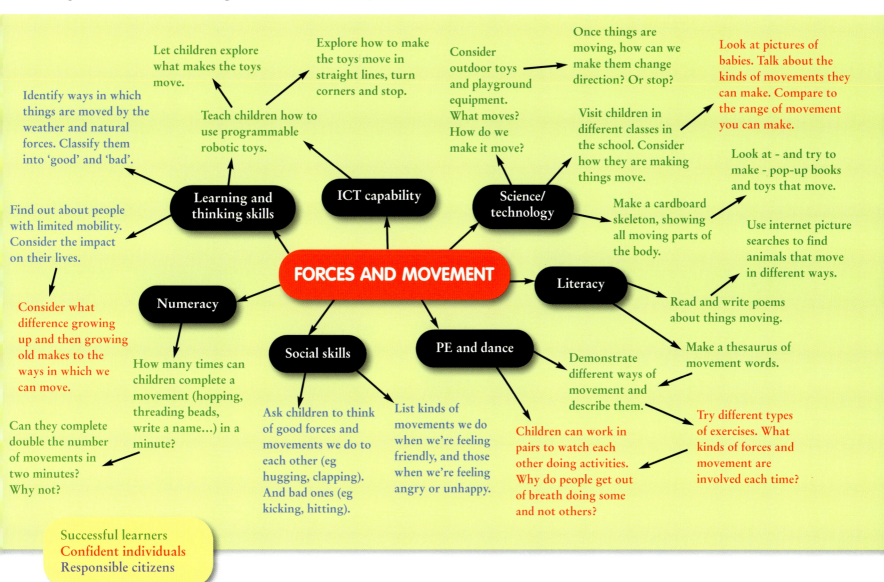

Let children explore what makes the toys move.

Explore how to make the toys move in straight lines, turn corners and stop.

Consider outdoor toys and playground equipment. What moves? How do we make it move?

Once things are moving, how can we make them change direction? Or stop?

Look at pictures of babies. Talk about the kinds of movements they can make. Compare to the range of movement you can make.

Identify ways in which things are moved by the weather and natural forces. Classify them into 'good' and 'bad'.

Teach children how to use programmable robotic toys.

Visit children in different classes in the school. Consider how they are making things move.

Look at - and try to make - pop-up books and toys that move.

Learning and thinking skills

ICT capability

Science/ technology

Make a cardboard skeleton, showing all moving parts of the body.

Use internet picture searches to find animals that move in different ways.

Find out about people with limited mobility. Consider the impact on their lives.

FORCES AND MOVEMENT

Literacy

Read and write poems about things moving.

Consider what difference growing up and then growing old makes to the ways in which we can move.

Numeracy

How many times can children complete a movement (hopping, threading beads, write a name...) in a minute?

Social skills

PE and dance

Demonstrate different ways of movement and describe them.

Make a thesaurus of movement words.

Can they complete double the number of movements in two minutes? Why not?

Ask children to think of good forces and movements we do to each other (eg hugging, clapping). And bad ones (eg kicking, hitting).

List kinds of movements we do when we're feeling friendly, and those when we're feeling angry or unhappy.

Children can work in pairs to watch each other doing activities. Why do people get out of breath doing some and not others?

Try different types of exercises. What kinds of forces and movement are involved each time?

Successful learners
Confident individuals
Responsible citizens

23

Index